THE
ADHD
3-DAY
SPRINT
WORKBOOK

curveball
PRESS

Jennifer Dall Ed.D

The ADHD 3-Day Sprint Workbook / Jennifer Dall Ed.D —1st ed.

Paperback ISBN: 979-8-9952108-0-1

THE ADHD 3-DAY SPRINT

WORKBOOK

JENNIFER DALL, Ed.D.

WELCOME TO *THE ADHD 3-DAY SPRINT WORKBOOK*

Hello, I'm your guide, Jennifer Dall, and I have ADHD. For so long, I struggled to consistently finish projects and stay on task. I would dive in, underestimate time and capacity, and allow other tasks to pop up and distract me. I read about people using extended three-week or three-month blocks to focus on work but knew that my ADHD brain needed to tackle projects in smaller bits. I sat with this idea and realized I needed smaller blocks of time to find success. I experimented and discovered that a 3-day sprint is perfect for this ADHD brain and for others who crave a way to manage tasks in small bites.

After testing a bit, I created The ADHD 3-Day Sprint method to help others learn to prioritize goals and allow time for a deep focus to successfully complete projects. Once you do one sprint, it will quickly become one of your favorite organizational tools.

Okay, enough yapping, let's get into how it works!

What exactly is The ADHD 3-Day Sprint and how does it work?

The ADHD 3-Day Sprint is a way to structure your work on projects so that you feel confident in starting a project and meet your goals.

During The ADHD 3-Day Sprint, you simply select a project, break down the tasks, and commit to completing each of the micro steps for that project over a specific 3-day period.

Science shows that ADHD brains struggle with issues such as *time blindness* (not realizing how long things take or how long the person has been working), *now vs. not now* (a vague understanding of time that is not immediate), and poor *executive function skills* (such as organization and prioritization).

This short time frame will fuel your creations and lead you to multiple small successes instead of overwhelming you with unmanageable larger goals. The goal is not perfectionism. Instead, it's about completing your sprint while being compassionate with yourself.

What Types of Projects Can You Do During an ADHD 3-Day Sprint?

The ADHD 3-Day Sprint can be for work or for fun.

Have a report or proposal to write? Want to create a photo exhibit or work on your novel? Need to plan or pack for a trip? Ready to fine-tune your house? Do something you dread like organizing all your papers, your taxes, or your kitchen cupboards?

The key to The ADHD 3-Day Sprint is to choose a goal that feels achievable in the course of 3 days. For example, if you are writing a book, focus on completing one chapter in the next 3 days. Or if you feel scattered about a lot of general life organization, maybe you tackle a certain room or area of your house over 3 days. The ADHD 3-Day Sprint is helpful for short-term projects or breaking bigger projects into smaller steps.

The best part is that framing your project in a 3-day block keeps things from taking up both physical and mental space during the rest of the week. It doesn't mean you can't do other projects, but you recognize that you have 3 days to complete a certain project and can better focus on it.

When Can You Do an ADHD 3-Day Sprint?

Anytime! Yes, really! Personally, I use this method almost every week, because it really helps me realistically focus on and feel success in my accomplishments. It also helps me focus on tasks I tend to want to put off.

However, you can do this once a month, for specific projects, or when you need to kickstart or reinvigorate yourself or a project.

The Steps of The ADHD 3-Day Sprint

STEP 1: THE BRAIN DUMP

Remember this: Your brain is a processor, not a storage facility!

Before you begin, it's good to get everything out of your head and onto paper.

This is especially helpful if you feel like you have so many ideas and details floating around in your head, and you don't know where to start.

Set a timer for a minute or two and write down every idea, detail, question, or step that you have or need to do. If you think of something that doesn't seem to fit within this project—write it down anyway! You will be able to think and work so much better once you get all the stray details on paper.

Think you've written it all down? Take a breath, shake your head, and see what else falls out!

Review your list. Some of these items don't fit in with your 3-day sprint? You can cross them off or move them to another list.

STEP 2: SET YOUR GOAL

Now it's time to narrow down your ADHD 3-Day Sprint topic. Consider these questions:

Can this project be accomplished in **one** 3-day sprint? Or is it a longer-term endeavor that will take many sprints—such as writing a book or larger paper, cleaning out a large portion of your house, or batching newsletters for your business?

Do you have several mini projects that can be combined into one ADHD 3-Day Sprint—such as paying the bills, editing a chapter, and cleaning out the fridge? Or writing a podcast script, going through your closet, and planning next week's menus?

Or some combination of any or all of the above?

Recently, I wanted to spend 2 hours each day writing a chapter of my novel and also spend a little bit of time each day completing some other tasks like refining my elevator speech, reviewing comments on a Tiny Book I'm writing, and studying some craft lessons from a writing group I am part of. So each day had a fiction writing task and one of the others. The combination worked well for me and might for you, too.

Most importantly, get honest with yourself and consider how much time you have to devote over the week **and** each

individual day. Do you have any appointments, scheduled meetings, or personal plans? Are you starting to feel worn out and don't want to get sick? Do you only have time on Monday, Thursday, and Saturday? Do you have 5 hours each day or 4 hours one day and then only 2 hours the other days? Is there a deadline that must be met no matter what? Can you build a cushion for life's little surprises? Those curveballs that come out of nowhere?

Once you have clarity, set your goal!

STEP 3: 3-DAY AT A GLANCE

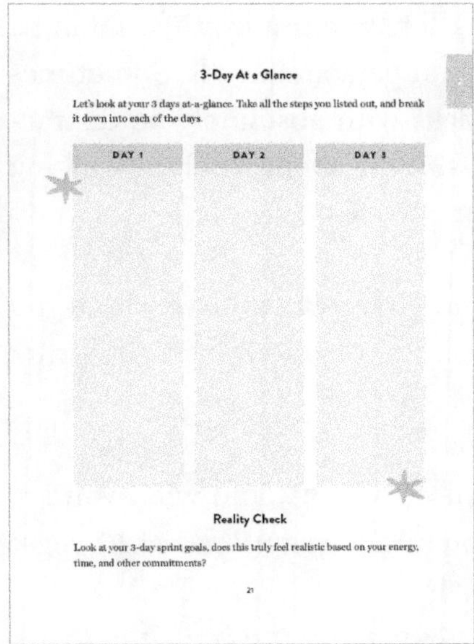

After you brainstorm all the ideas, tasks, thoughts, and steps on paper, it's time to narrow down your specific goal and create an overview of what's to come. Remember, you are working for 3 days with the time that you have available. This is your road-map for the 3-day sprint.

As much as possible, I like each day to have a contained task or subtask. I like to start by completing this statement: *"By the end of to-day I will..."* What can I accomplish in the 2 or 4 hours I have this day? And the second day? And then on the final day?

And finally, write down the steps in order. When you are busy, dealing with curveballs, or are neurodivergent, it can be very easy to skip over steps. You know you, and you know how detailed you need to be. Take a look and see if the steps flow logically or if you are missing something.

When you first begin this process, you might ask someone to review your steps. In middle school, I had to write out the steps for making a PB&J sandwich and then read them to another person who had to follow the steps—omissions became very apparent!

STEP 4: BEGIN THE ADHD 3-DAY SPRINT

Each day of the 3-Day sprint you will fill out your daily sheet. Write your daily goal, so it is top of mind. Then write down the main steps and beware of stacking too many. Research has shown that you can really only complete around 3 or 4 tasks in a day. Perhaps each task is very small and you can complete 5 or 6. Perhaps they are big and you have time for 1 or 2. Even with some bigger tasks, you might consider breaking those down into more manageable steps. Remember the aim is successful completion, not doing it all in one day!

Next, block off the specific time you have on the calendar. Is it from 8-10 am? 9-11 am and then 7-9 pm? For that day, block off the time. I suggest using short blocks such as the Pomodoro Method—working for 25 minutes, then taking a 5-minute break to stretch your legs and take care of personal needs. Sometimes I work best in one- or two-hour deep-focus blocks with absolutely no distractions. Do you have appointments, meetings, calls? How about meals or walking the dog? Consider all the possibilities of your time blocks.

At the end of the day, take a moment to check in. First, take note of where you left off, especially if you are continuing this task tomorrow. You might write: *Edited 10 pages, still need to edit the last 5 pages.*

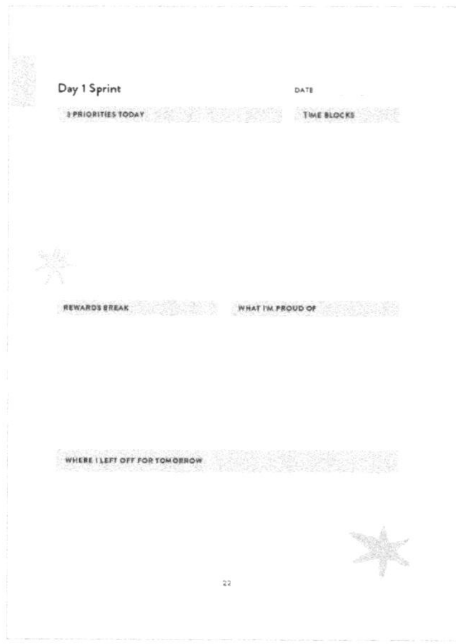

Note your success, wins, and what you are proud of. You might write: *I edited 10 pages today! I worked 4 hours. I took a break every 25 minutes to move my body and drink a glass of water.*

A friendly reminder: Sometimes you might get off track and that's okay. Today fell apart? Well, you still have two more days to get back on track. You may need to alter your final goal, but you have a clear path to pick yourself back up, brush your bum off, and keep going.

STEP 5: REFLECTION

The final step of your ADHD 3-Day Sprint can be done at the conclusion of the 3rd day—or the following day—but please don't forget to do this! Take a moment and look back over your daily planning sheets and your finished work.

No matter whether you finished it all or not, be kind to yourself! You did work, you did your best, you did what you could in these 3 days. Take time to answer:

My sprint goals were:

My success/completed tasks were:

What didn't work well this sprint:

Next steps, things to continue, what to try different next time:

Take this information with you when you do your next ADHD 3-Day Sprint, so you can see what worked or what didn't work and can improve.

Now It's Your Turn

In this workbook, you will find 12 weeks (or 3 months) worth of ADHD 3-Day Sprints. You can grab the workbook and do sprints as needed for certain projects or times in your life, or you can use them for a bigger project and do sprints weekly over the course of 3 months.

Want to add some fun? Consider finding a way to get out of town—or at least the house—and do your ADHD 3-Day Sprint in a hotel, rental house, or with a buddy, with all the obligations of life packed away for a while.

The ADHD 3-Day Sprint is a process and, no matter what you accomplish, you are a success because of it. You are closer to your goals than you were before and that's what counts! It's a process to accurately plan out and hold on to your time, no matter what life, outsiders, and curveballs beyond your control come your way. You got this, and I'm rooting for you!

The Brain Dump

**Get everything out of your mind so that there
are no distractions later.**

What is Your Goal?

What are the steps to meet that goal? List them out.

3-Day At a Glance

Let's look at your 3 days at-a-glance. Take all the steps you listed out, and break it down into each of the days.

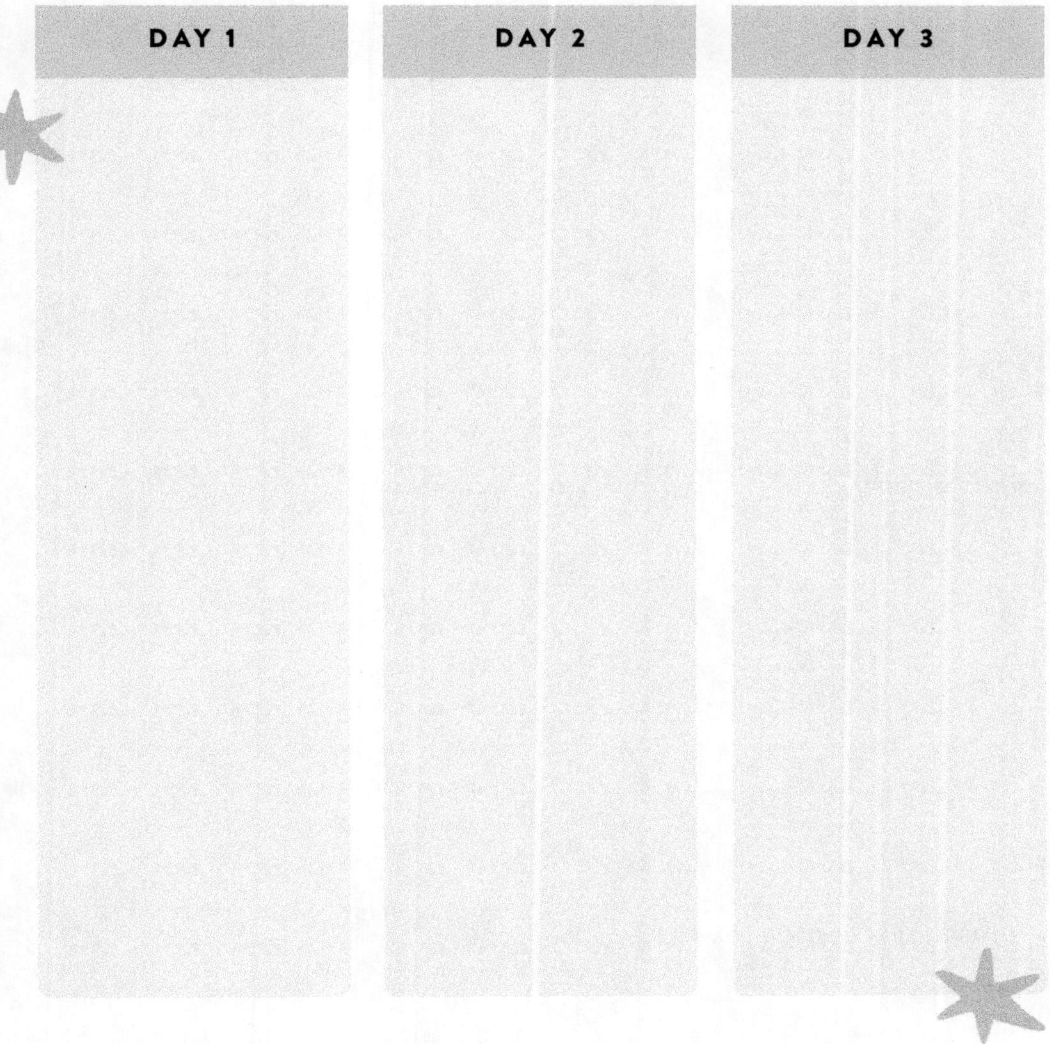

Reality Check

Look at your 3-day sprint goals, does this truly feel realistic based on your energy, time, and other commitments?

Day 1 Sprint

DATE ______________________

3 PRIORITIES TODAY

TIME BLOCKS

REWARDS BREAK

WHAT I'M PROUD OF

WHERE I LEFT OFF FOR TOMORROW

Day 2 Sprint

DATE ___________________

3 PRIORITIES TODAY

TIME BLOCKS

REWARDS BREAK

WHAT I'M PROUD OF

WHERE I LEFT OFF FOR TOMORROW

Day 3 Sprint

3 PRIORITIES TODAY

TIME BLOCKS

REWARDS BREAK

WHAT I'M PROUD OF

WHAT STILL NEEDS DONE TO COMPLETE THIS PROJECT

Reflection

List sprint goals, what you accomplished, and then reflect on some questions like: What worked well? What might you change? What's next? Do you need to do another sprint?

The Brain Dump

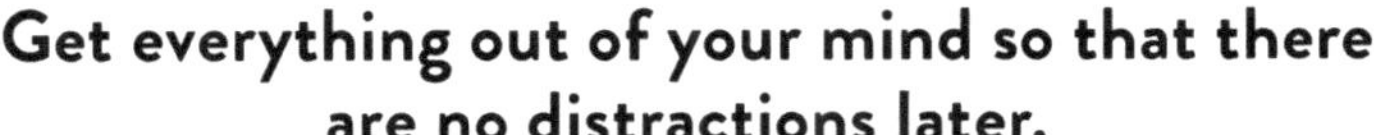

**Get everything out of your mind so that there
are no distractions later.**

What is Your Goal?

What are the steps to meet that goal? List them out.

3-Day At a Glance

Let's look at your 3 days at-a-glance. Take all the steps you listed out, and break it down into each of the days.

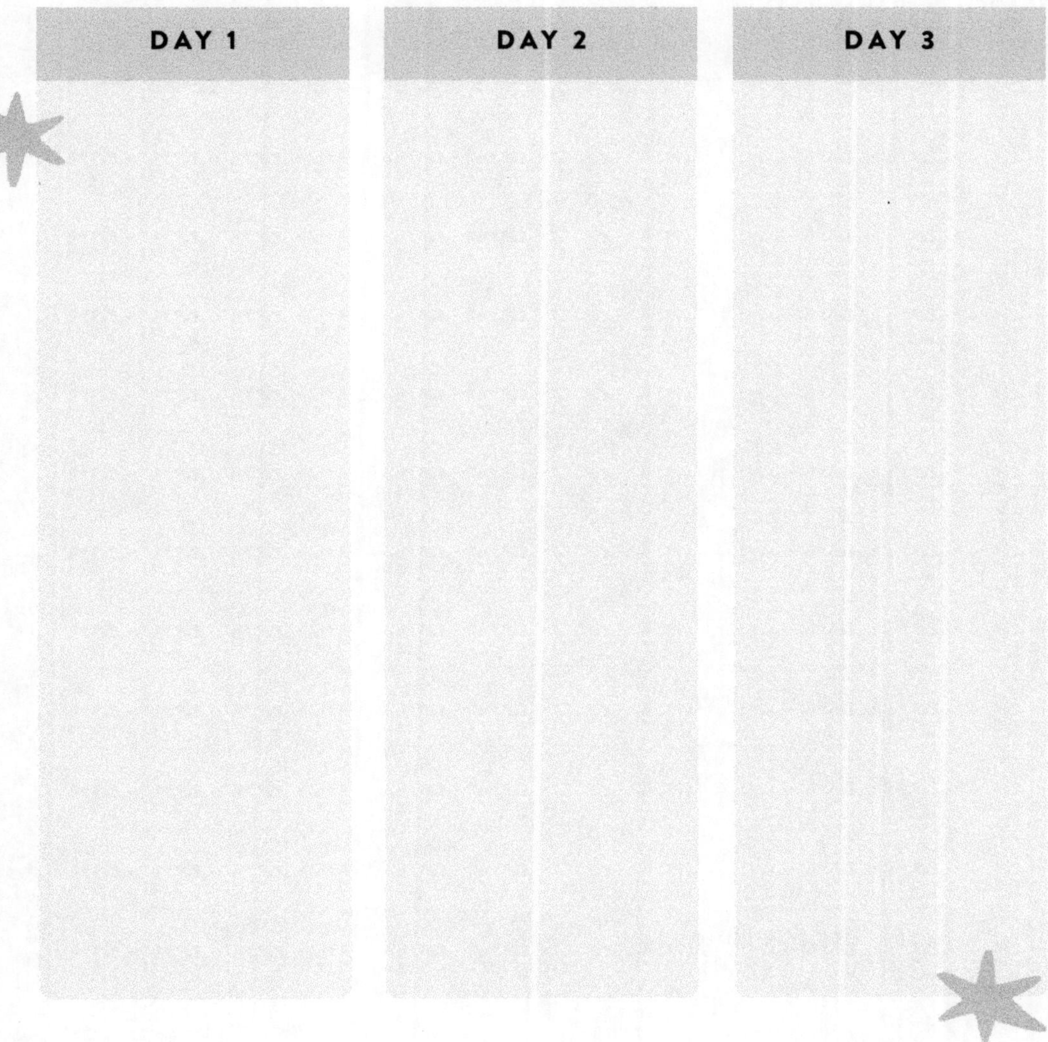

Reality Check

Look at your 3-day sprint goals, does this truly feel realistic based on your energy, time, and other commitments?

Day 1 Sprint

DATE ________________________

Day 2 Sprint

DATE _______________

3 PRIORITIES TODAY

TIME BLOCKS

REWARDS BREAK

WHAT I'M PROUD OF

WHERE I LEFT OFF FOR TOMORROW

Day 3 Sprint

DATE _______________________

3 PRIORITIES TODAY

TIME BLOCKS

REWARDS BREAK

WHAT I'M PROUD OF

WHAT STILL NEEDS DONE TO COMPLETE THIS PROJECT

Reflection

List sprint goals, what you accomplished, and then reflect on some questions like:
What worked well? What might you change? What's next? Do you need to do
another sprint?

The Brain Dump

**Get everything out of your mind so that there
are no distractions later.**

What is Your Goal?

What are the steps to meet that goal? List them out.

3-Day At a Glance

Let's look at your 3 days at-a-glance. Take all the steps you listed out, and break it down into each of the days.

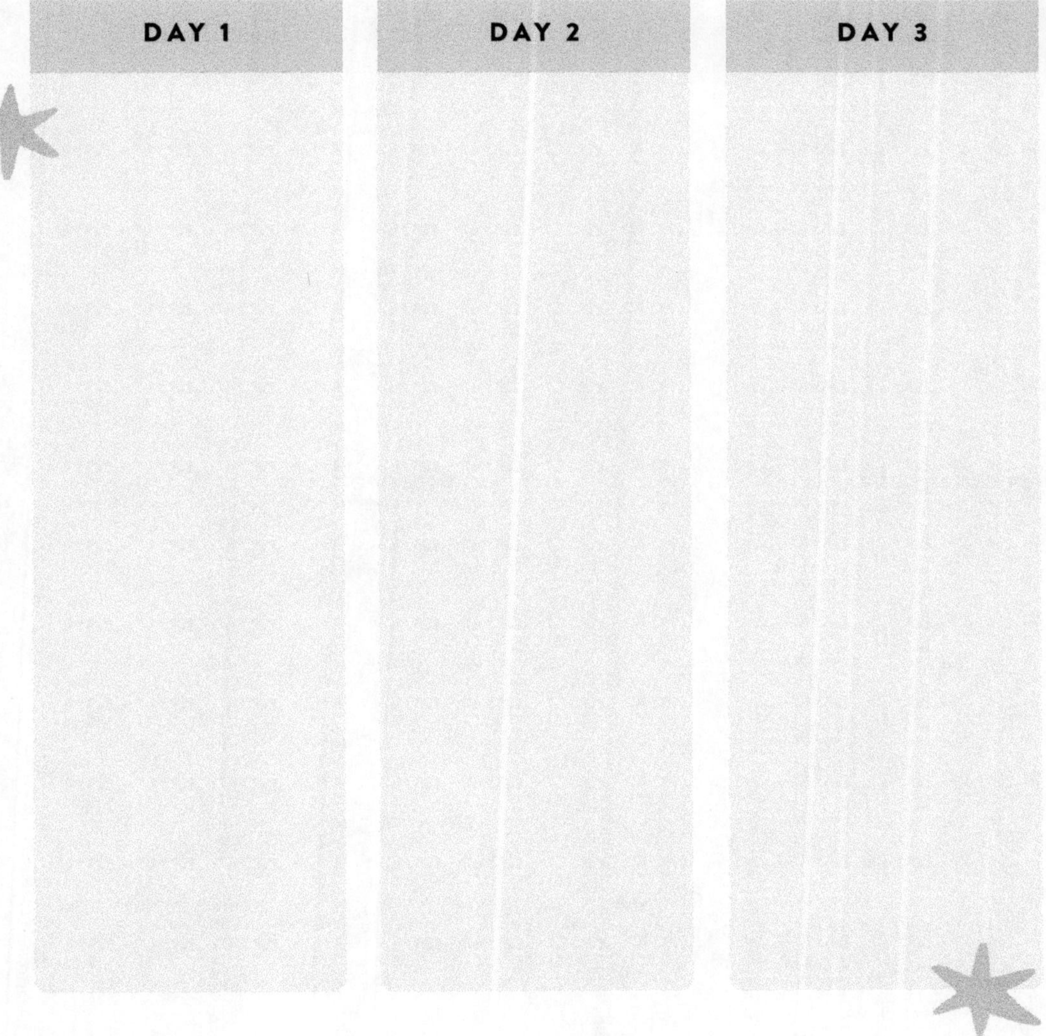

Reality Check

Look at your 3-day sprint goals, does this truly feel realistic based on your energy, time, and other commitments?

Day 1 Sprint

3 PRIORITIES TODAY

TIME BLOCKS

REWARDS BREAK

WHAT I'M PROUD OF

WHERE I LEFT OFF FOR TOMORROW

Day 2 Sprint

DATE ________________________

3 PRIORITIES TODAY

TIME BLOCKS

3

REWARDS BREAK

WHAT I'M PROUD OF

WHERE I LEFT OFF FOR TOMORROW

Day 3 Sprint

3 PRIORITIES TODAY

TIME BLOCKS

REWARDS BREAK

WHAT I'M PROUD OF

WHAT STILL NEEDS DONE TO COMPLETE THIS PROJECT

Reflection

List sprint goals, what you accomplished, and then reflect on some questions like:
What worked well? What might you change? What's next? Do you need to do
another sprint?

The Brain Dump

Get everything out of your mind so that there
are no distractions later.

What is Your Goal?

What are the steps to meet that goal? List them out.

3-Day At a Glance

Let's look at your 3 days at-a-glance. Take all the steps you listed out, and break it down into each of the days.

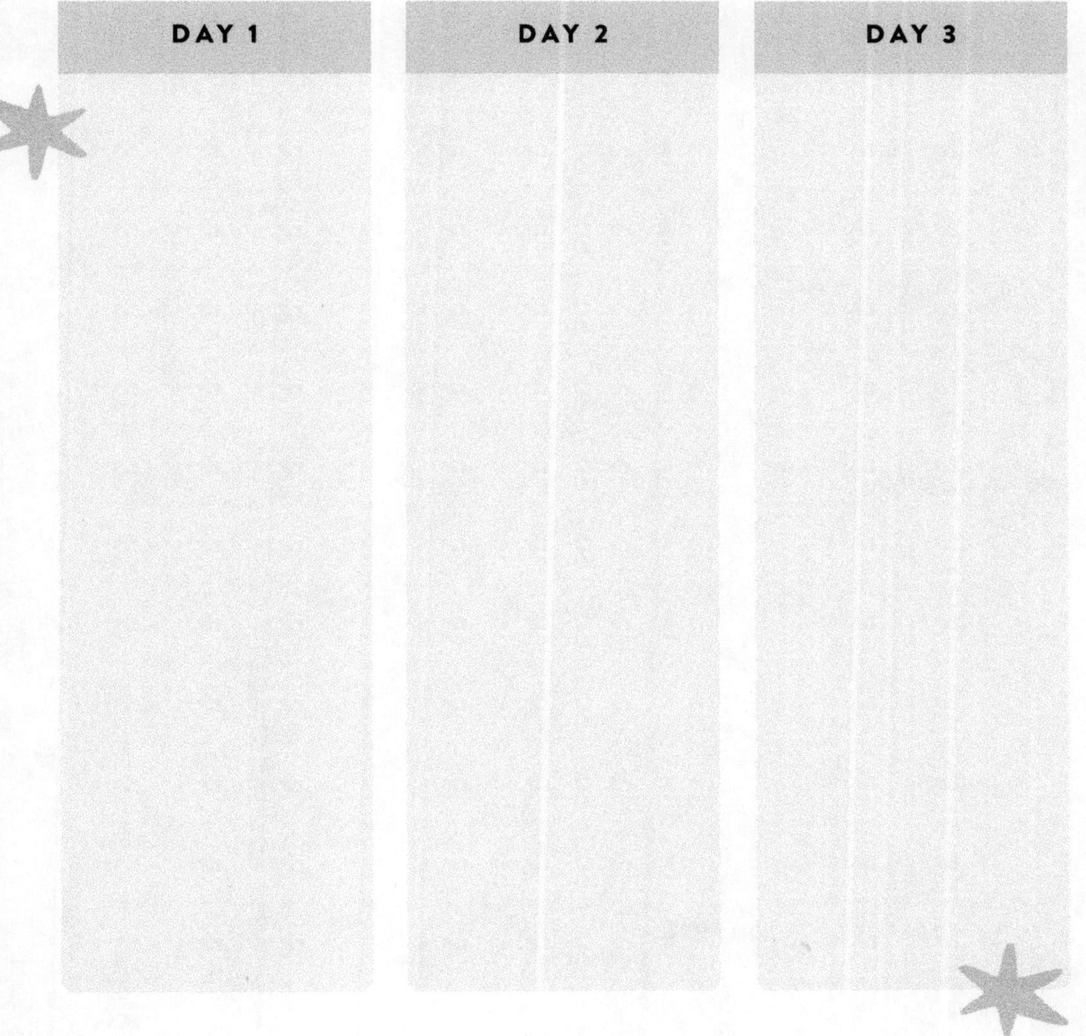

Reality Check

Look at your 3-day sprint goals, does this truly feel realistic based on your energy, time, and other commitments?

Day 1 Sprint

DATE _______________

3 PRIORITIES TODAY

TIME BLOCKS

REWARDS BREAK

WHAT I'M PROUD OF

WHERE I LEFT OFF FOR TOMORROW

Day 2 Sprint

DATE ______________________

3 PRIORITIES TODAY

TIME BLOCKS

REWARDS BREAK

WHAT I'M PROUD OF

WHERE I LEFT OFF FOR TOMORROW

Day 3 Sprint

DATE ________________

Reflection

List sprint goals, what you accomplished, and then reflect on some questions like:
What worked well? What might you change? What's next? Do you need to do
another sprint?

The Brain Dump

**Get everything out of your mind so that there
are no distractions later.**

What is Your Goal?

What are the steps to meet that goal? List them out.

3-Day At a Glance

Let's look at your 3 days at-a-glance. Take all the steps you listed out, and break it down into each of the days.

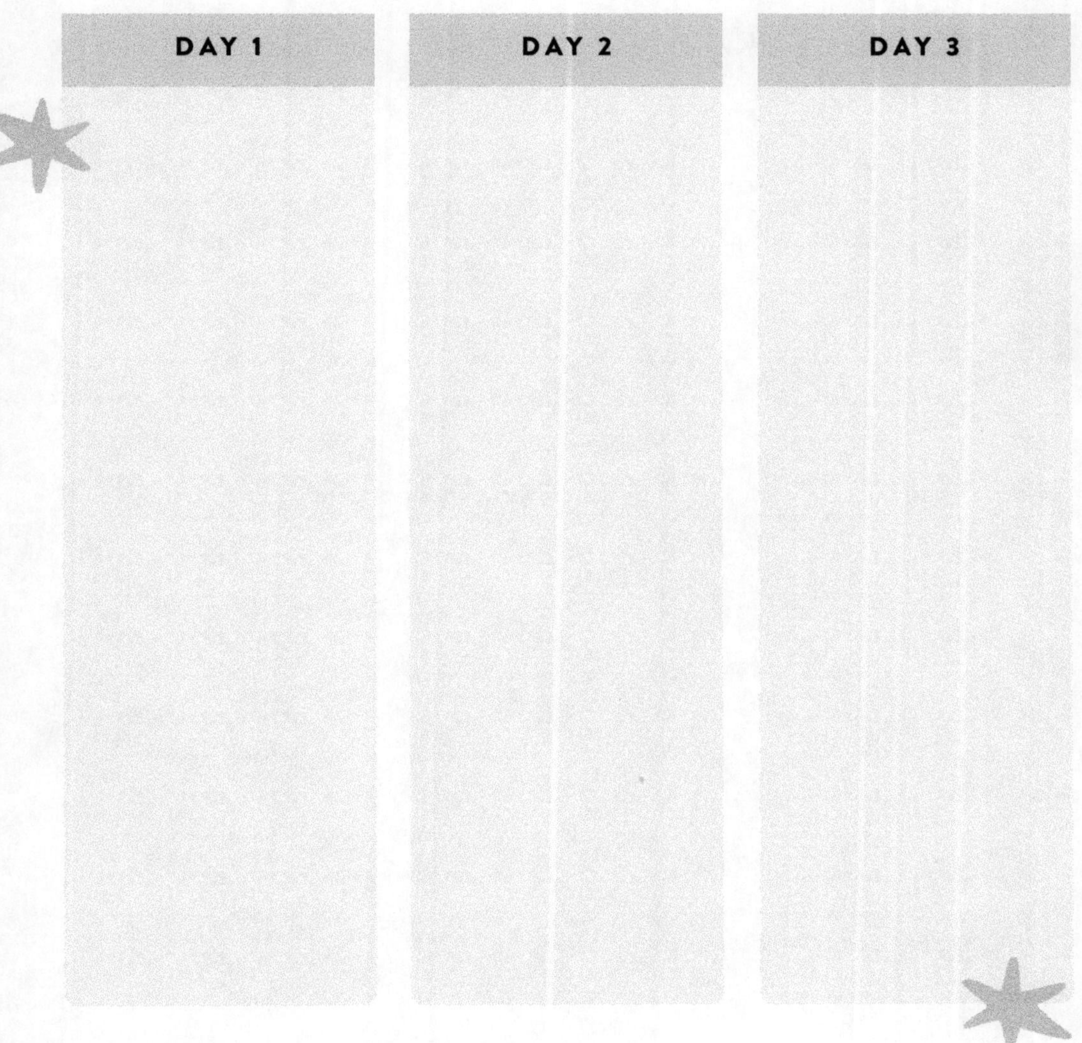

Reality Check

Look at your 3-day sprint goals, does this truly feel realistic based on your energy, time, and other commitments?

Day 1 Sprint

3 PRIORITIES TODAY

TIME BLOCKS

REWARDS BREAK

WHAT I'M PROUD OF

WHERE I LEFT OFF FOR TOMORROW

Day 2 Sprint

DATE ___________________

3 PRIORITIES TODAY

TIME BLOCKS

REWARDS BREAK

WHAT I'M PROUD OF

WHERE I LEFT OFF FOR TOMORROW

Day 3 Sprint

3 PRIORITIES TODAY

TIME BLOCKS

REWARDS BREAK

WHAT I'M PROUD OF

WHAT STILL NEEDS DONE TO COMPLETE THIS PROJECT

Reflection

List sprint goals, what you accomplished, and then reflect on some questions like: What worked well? What might you change? What's next? Do you need to do another sprint?

The Brain Dump

**Get everything out of your mind so that there
are no distractions later.**

What is Your Goal?

What are the steps to meet that goal? List them out.

3-Day At a Glance

Let's look at your 3 days at-a-glance. Take all the steps you listed out, and break it down into each of the days.

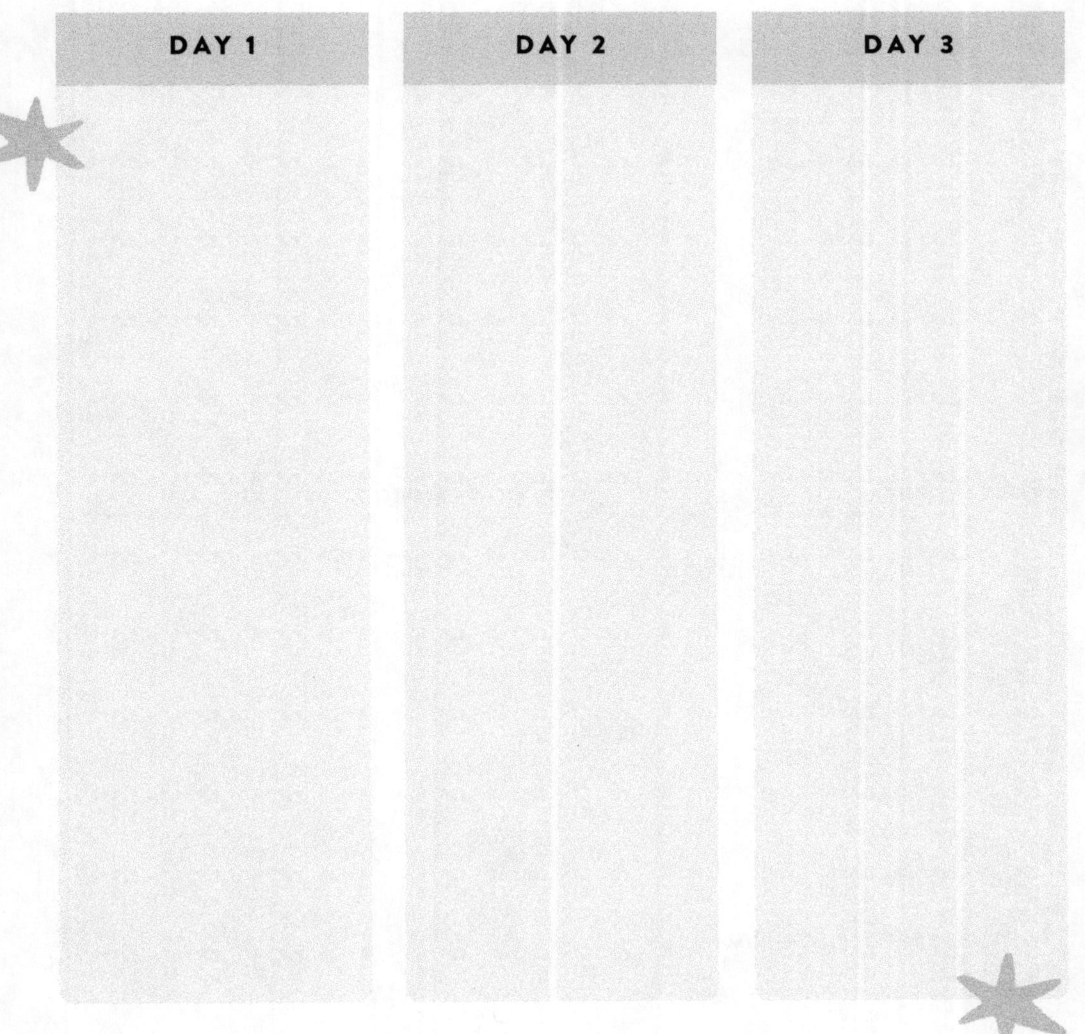

Reality Check

Look at your 3-day sprint goals, does this truly feel realistic based on your energy, time, and other commitments?

Day 1 Sprint

DATE ___________________

Day 2 Sprint

DATE ________________

3 PRIORITIES TODAY

TIME BLOCKS

REWARDS BREAK

WHAT I'M PROUD OF

WHERE I LEFT OFF FOR TOMORROW

Day 3 Sprint

3 PRIORITIES TODAY

TIME BLOCKS

REWARDS BREAK

WHAT I'M PROUD OF

WHAT STILL NEEDS DONE TO COMPLETE THIS PROJECT

Reflection

List sprint goals, what you accomplished, and then reflect on some questions like:
What worked well? What might you change? What's next? Do you need to do
another sprint?

The Brain Dump

**Get everything out of your mind so that there
are no distractions later.**

What is Your Goal?

What are the steps to meet that goal? List them out.

3-Day At a Glance

Let's look at your 3 days at-a-glance. Take all the steps you listed out, and break it down into each of the days.

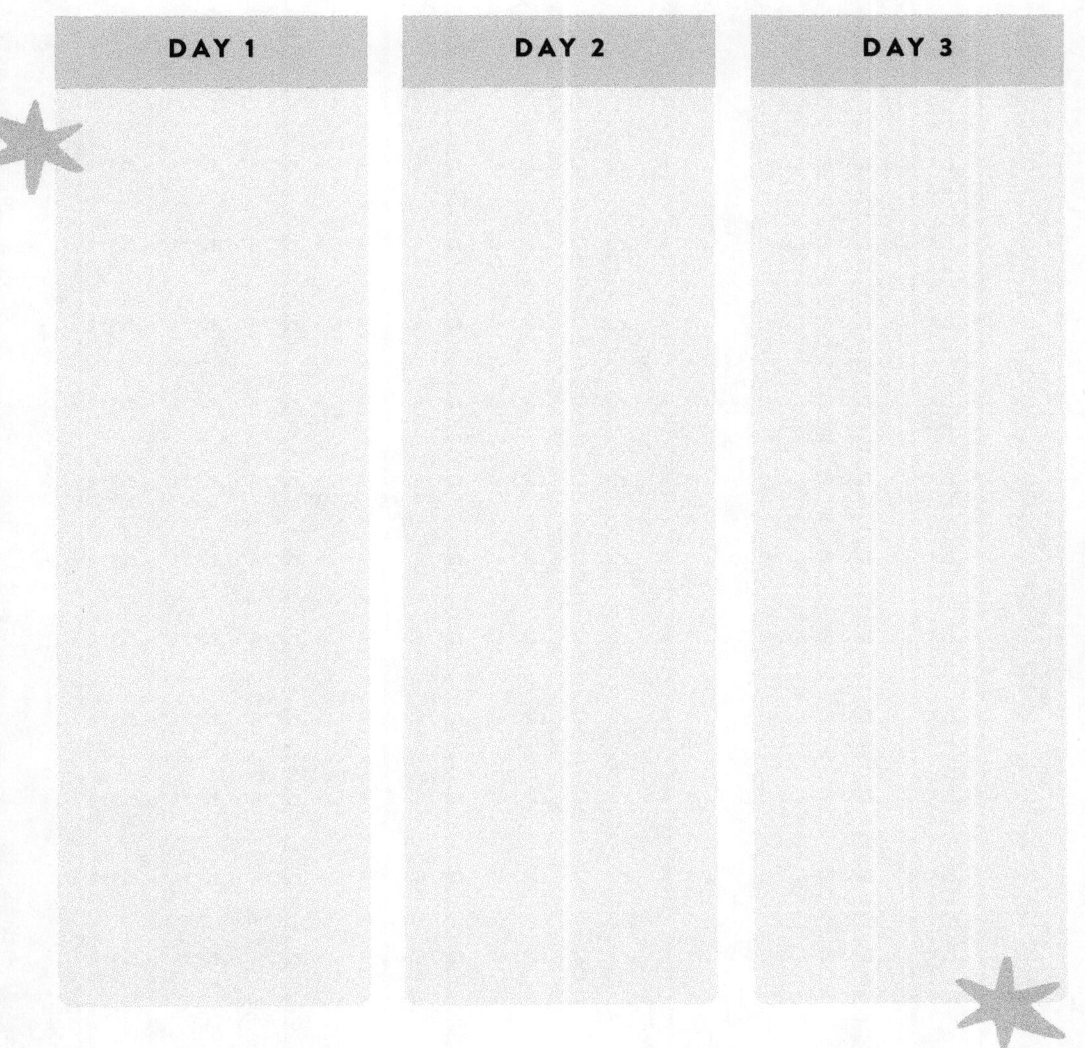

Reality Check

Look at your 3-day sprint goals, does this truly feel realistic based on your energy, time, and other commitments?

Day 1 Sprint

DATE _______________

3 PRIORITIES TODAY

TIME BLOCKS

REWARDS BREAK

WHAT I'M PROUD OF

WHERE I LEFT OFF FOR TOMORROW

Day 2 Sprint

DATE ___________________

3 PRIORITIES TODAY

TIME BLOCKS

REWARDS BREAK

WHAT I'M PROUD OF

WHERE I LEFT OFF FOR TOMORROW

Day 3 Sprint

3 PRIORITIES TODAY

TIME BLOCKS

REWARDS BREAK

WHAT I'M PROUD OF

WHAT STILL NEEDS DONE TO COMPLETE THIS PROJECT

Reflection

List sprint goals, what you accomplished, and then reflect on some questions like: What worked well? What might you change? What's next? Do you need to do another sprint?

The Brain Dump

**Get everything out of your mind so that there
are no distractions later.**

What is Your Goal?

What are the steps to meet that goal? List them out.

3-Day At a Glance

Let's look at your 3 days at-a-glance. Take all the steps you listed out, and break it down into each of the days.

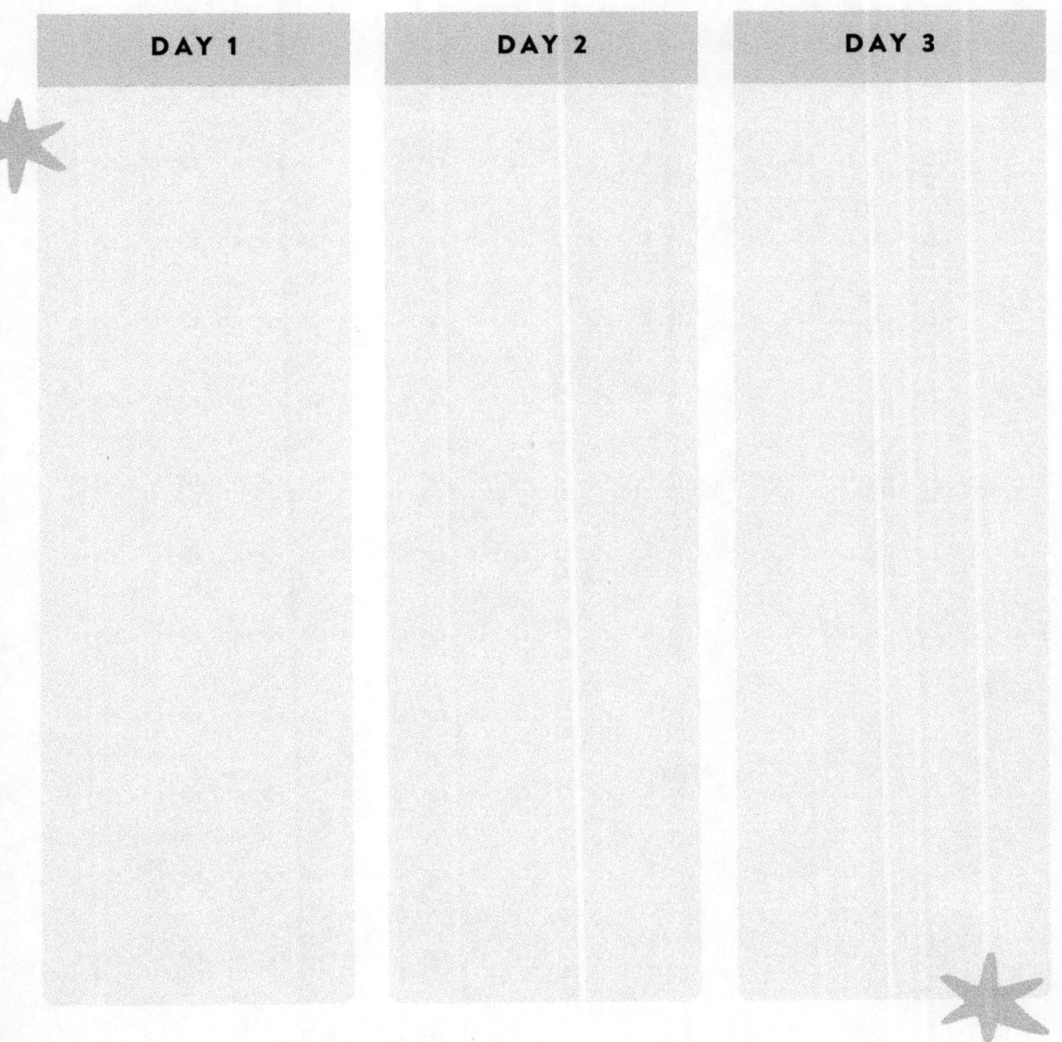

Reality Check

Look at your 3-day sprint goals, does this truly feel realistic based on your energy, time, and other commitments?

Day 1 Sprint

3 PRIORITIES TODAY

TIME BLOCKS

REWARDS BREAK

WHAT I'M PROUD OF

WHERE I LEFT OFF FOR TOMORROW

Day 2 Sprint

DATE _______________

3 PRIORITIES TODAY

TIME BLOCKS

REWARDS BREAK

WHAT I'M PROUD OF

WHERE I LEFT OFF FOR TOMORROW

Day 3 Sprint

DATE ______________

3 PRIORITIES TODAY

TIME BLOCKS

REWARDS BREAK

WHAT I'M PROUD OF

WHAT STILL NEEDS DONE TO COMPLETE THIS PROJECT

Reflection

List sprint goals, what you accomplished, and then reflect on some questions like: What worked well? What might you change? What's next? Do you need to do another sprint?

The Brain Dump

Get everything out of your mind so that there are no distractions later.

What is Your Goal?

What are the steps to meet that goal? List them out.

3-Day At a Glance

Let's look at your 3 days at-a-glance. Take all the steps you listed out, and break it down into each of the days.

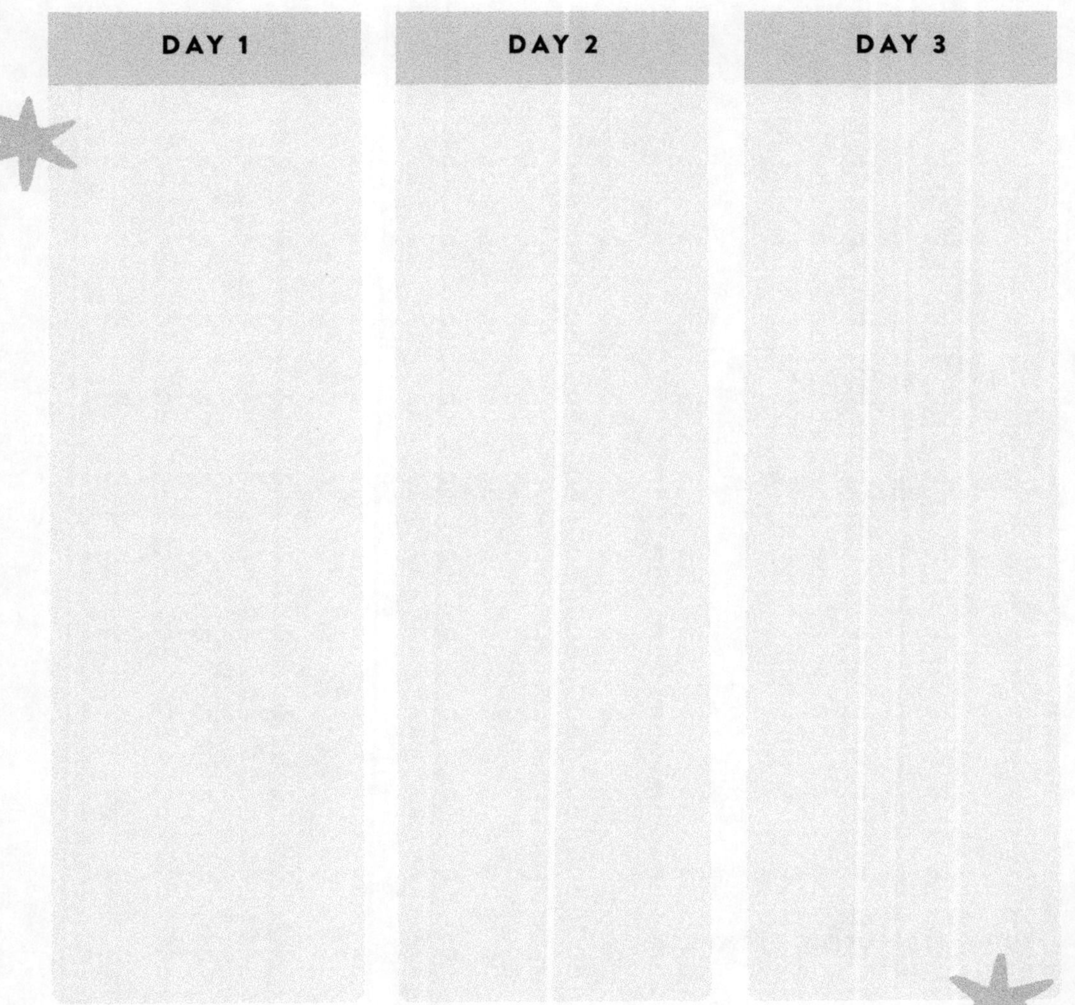

Reality Check

Look at your 3-day sprint goals, does this truly feel realistic based on your energy, time, and other commitments?

Day 1 Sprint

3 PRIORITIES TODAY

TIME BLOCKS

REWARDS BREAK

WHAT I'M PROUD OF

WHERE I LEFT OFF FOR TOMORROW

Day 2 Sprint

DATE ________________

3 PRIORITIES TODAY

TIME BLOCKS

REWARDS BREAK

WHAT I'M PROUD OF

WHERE I LEFT OFF FOR TOMORROW

9

Day 3 Sprint

3 PRIORITIES TODAY

TIME BLOCKS

REWARDS BREAK

WHAT I'M PROUD OF

WHAT STILL NEEDS DONE TO COMPLETE THIS PROJECT

Reflection

List sprint goals, what you accomplished, and then reflect on some questions like: What worked well? What might you change? What's next? Do you need to do another sprint?

The Brain Dump

Get everything out of your mind so that there
are no distractions later.

What is Your Goal?

What are the steps to meet that goal? List them out.

3-Day At a Glance

Let's look at your 3 days at-a-glance. Take all the steps you listed out, and break it down into each of the days.

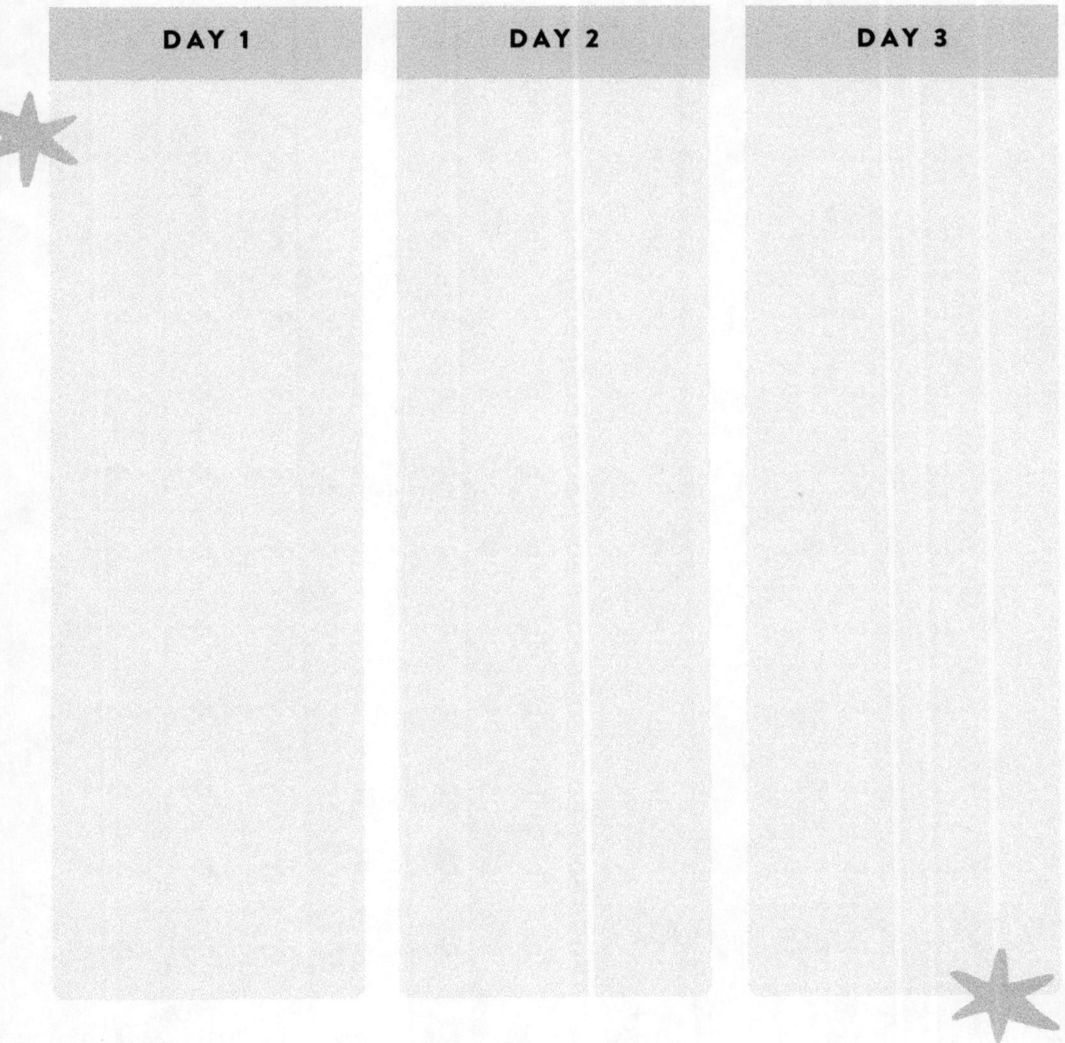

Reality Check

Look at your 3-day sprint goals, does this truly feel realistic based on your energy, time, and other commitments?

Day 1 Sprint

3 PRIORITIES TODAY

TIME BLOCKS

REWARDS BREAK

WHAT I'M PROUD OF

WHERE I LEFT OFF FOR TOMORROW

Day 2 Sprint

DATE ______________________

10

Day 3 Sprint

DATE _______________

3 PRIORITIES TODAY

TIME BLOCKS

REWARDS BREAK

WHAT I'M PROUD OF

WHAT STILL NEEDS DONE TO COMPLETE THIS PROJECT

Reflection

List sprint goals, what you accomplished, and then reflect on some questions like: What worked well? What might you change? What's next? Do you need to do another sprint?

The Brain Dump

Get everything out of your mind so that there
are no distractions later.

11

What is Your Goal?

What are the steps to meet that goal? List them out.

3-Day At a Glance

Let's look at your 3 days at-a-glance. Take all the steps you listed out, and break it down into each of the days.

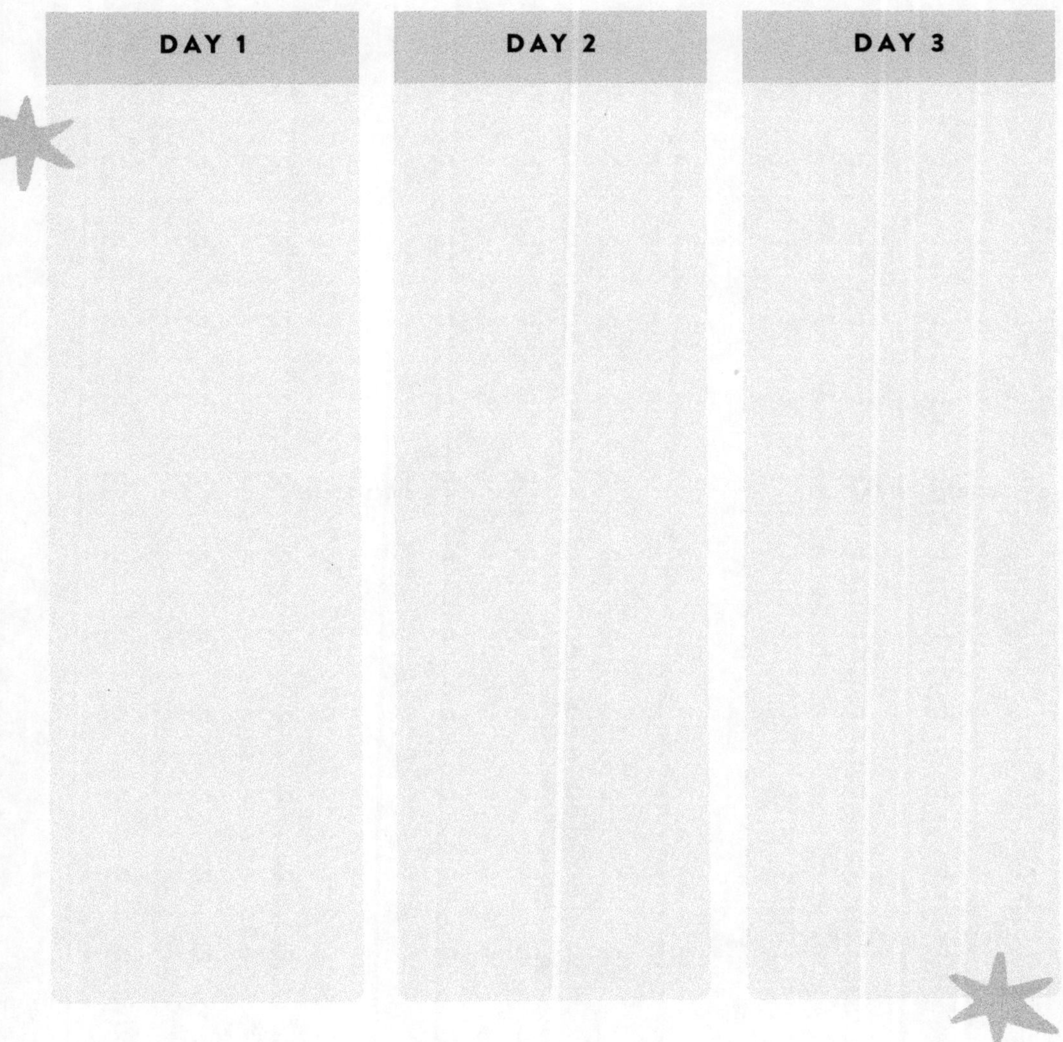

Reality Check

Look at your 3-day sprint goals, does this truly feel realistic based on your energy, time, and other commitments?

Day 1 Sprint

DATE ___________________

3 PRIORITIES TODAY

TIME BLOCKS

REWARDS BREAK

WHAT I'M PROUD OF

WHERE I LEFT OFF FOR TOMORROW

Day 2 Sprint

DATE ___________________

3 PRIORITIES TODAY

TIME BLOCKS

REWARDS BREAK

WHAT I'M PROUD OF

WHERE I LEFT OFF FOR TOMORROW

11

Day 3 Sprint

3 PRIORITIES TODAY

TIME BLOCKS

REWARDS BREAK

WHAT I'M PROUD OF

WHAT STILL NEEDS DONE TO COMPLETE THIS PROJECT

Reflection

List sprint goals, what you accomplished, and then reflect on some questions like: What worked well? What might you change? What's next? Do you need to do another sprint?

The Brain Dump

**Get everything out of your mind so that there
are no distractions later.**

What is Your Goal?

What are the steps to meet that goal? List them out.

3-Day At a Glance

Let's look at your 3 days at-a-glance. Take all the steps you listed out, and break it down into each of the days.

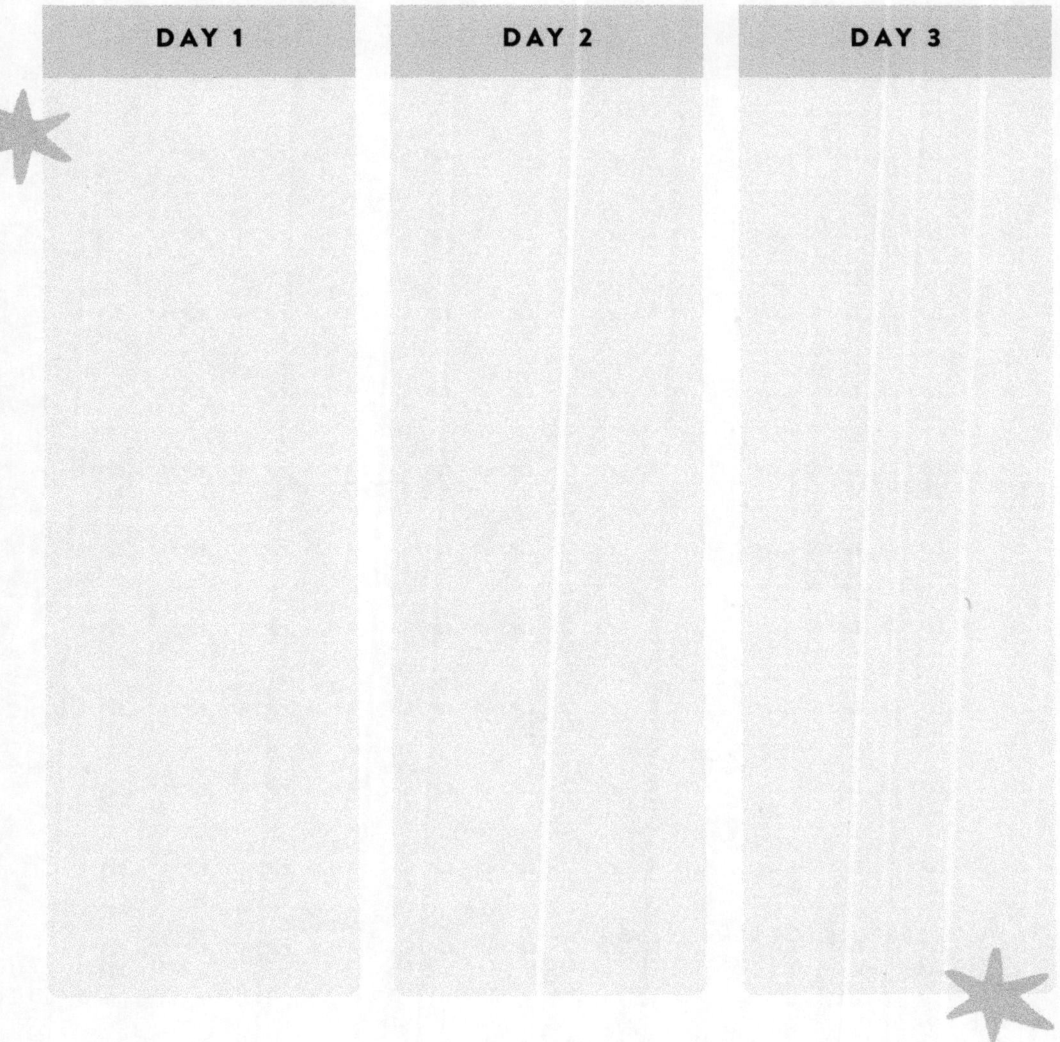

DAY 1	DAY 2	DAY 3

Reality Check

Look at your 3-day sprint goals, does this truly feel realistic based on your energy, time, and other commitments?

Day 1 Sprint

3 PRIORITIES TODAY

TIME BLOCKS

REWARDS BREAK

WHAT I'M PROUD OF

WHERE I LEFT OFF FOR TOMORROW

Day 2 Sprint

DATE ______________________

3 PRIORITIES TODAY

TIME BLOCKS

REWARDS BREAK

WHAT I'M PROUD OF

WHERE I LEFT OFF FOR TOMORROW

12

Day 3 Sprint

3 PRIORITIES TODAY

TIME BLOCKS

REWARDS BREAK

WHAT I'M PROUD OF

WHAT STILL NEEDS DONE TO COMPLETE THIS PROJECT

Reflection

List sprint goals, what you accomplished, and then reflect on some questions like:
What worked well? What might you change? What's next? Do you need to do
another sprint?